ANDERSHIRE BOOKS

< DRAFT VERSION >

Winning the War

God's Plan for Victory and the Defeat of Evil in this Present Age

NONFICTION BY

David Bard Kullberg

Winning the War
God's Plan for Victory and the Defeat of Evil in this Present Age

David Bard Kullberg

ANDERSHIRE BOOKS

Winning the War – God's Plan for Victory and the Defeat of Evil in this Present Age

Copyright © 2014 by David B. Kullberg. All rights reserved.

No part of this book may be reproduced or transmitted in any form or by any means, electronic or mechanical, including photocopying, recording, or by any information storage and retrieval system, without written permission from the author.

Website for information: http://waragainstgod.com
Requests for information: openskybooks@gmail.com

Cover Design by Pending

Publishing services provided by JFK Administrative Services, ltd. jfkadm@gmail.com

All Scripture quotations, unless otherwise indicated, are taken from the Holy Bible, New International Version (NIV). Copyright 1973, 1978, 1984 by the International Bible Society. Used by permission of Zondervan Publishing House. All rights reserved.

ISBN 978-0-9884321-3-0

Printed in the United States of America.

Dedicated to Nathaniel, Isaac, Ander, Gabriel, Sydney, Jonah and Loa, and to all grandchildren everywhere. May we live for God's glory and for your future.

A special thanks to Kelly, my wife and best friend. *Winning the War* would not have been completed without your encouragement, advice, support and perseverance. I am a most fortunate man.

Table of Contents

Introduction: A Call to Courage 1
   A Foundation of Shifting Sand 2
   Seeing the Story Differently 3
   Winning the War 4

Chapter 1: Does Our Vision of the Future Matter? 7
   Why Our Vision of the Future Matters 9
   Faithful Testimony 10
   Hope versus Resignation 12

Chapter 2. God Starts With the End in Mind 15

Chapter 3: Why Would God Allow Evil to Enter His Creation? 17

Chapter 4: What If Jesus Had All Authority? 21
   The Nature of Authority and Faith 23

Chapter 5: Continual Spiritual Warfare: Dispossessing the City of Man 27
   A Conqueror Bent on Conquest 29

Chapter 6: Satan Empowers the City of Man 31
   We Are Soldiers in the Battle 33
   Babylon – The Utopian Dream 35

Chapter 7: Babylon Falls 37
   Breaking Babylon's Spell 38

Chapter 8: Christ's Kingdom Rises 41
   The Gradual Growth of God's Kingdom 45
   Restoring Our Created Image 47

Chapter 9: The Last Battle: The Final Defeat of Satan and the Destruction of Evil 53
   A Parable of the Devil's Release 56
   The Stage is Set 58

Chapter 10: How to Live in This Story 65
   The Story Summary 65
   Where We Are in the Story 67
   Living Faithfully in the Story 69

Epilogue 73

Appendix A: Interpreting Biblical Metaphors 75

Appendix B: Attributes of the World System 77

Appendix C: The Kingdom's Growth to Predominance is Not a Theocracy 79

Appendix D: Three Common Theological Views of the Millennium 83

Acknowledgements 87

The War Against God 89

For C.S. Lewis, Christian faith was not merely a set of religious beliefs or institutional customs or moral traditions. It was rather the recognition of a profound cosmic drama, an ongoing struggle between good and evil – in unseen places, in our own workaday world and in every human heart.

~ David C. Downing, *Into the Region of Awe*

Introduction:
A Call to Courage

Is the decline of America inevitable? Is the erosion of our nation's biblical foundation the fulfillment of prophecy? During the 20th Century, many Christians came to believe that evil will grow stronger and the Church will be increasingly marginalized and persecuted until Jesus returns.

Winning the War rediscovers a different vision of the future. The powerful proclamations of Scripture are not words of withdrawal or defeat. Scripture conveys a confidence that victory, within the confines of history, is God's intended outcome.

Victory – not just after Christ's Second Coming, but also during this present age. Victory – not just in heaven, but especially on earth during this time. This is where Satan and the powers of evil challenge Christ's authority; therefore, this is where the battle must be won – and that is essentially what is happening. Jesus will remain in the heavenly realm, at the Father's right hand, *until he has put all his enemies under his feet* (1 Corinthians 15:25). He is calling His people to bold and faithful courage as we participate in this great story. Then he will return **after he has won the victory**.

When considering these issues of future events, one soon discovers significant disagreement among capable scholars regarding biblical interpretations. To wade into these debates as a layperson can be overwhelming. Yet despite differences of opinion about prophecy and the manifestation of God's kingdom on earth, orthodox scholars do agree that Jesus will return some day and renew all things. **That eventuality, though comforting, does not eliminate our need to understand what the future holds for God's people on earth during this present age – because what a person believes about the future shapes his or her reality and important life decisions made in the present.**

A Foundation of Shifting Sand

Many deeply distressed Americans are convinced our nation's culture is going from bad to worse. Unfortunately, these premonitions seem warranted. America has progressively become a nation resting on a foundation of shifting sand. "But everyone who hears these words of mine and does not put them into practice is like a foolish man who built his house on sand… [A]nd the winds blew and beat against that house, and it fell with a great crash" (Matthew 7:26-27).

The pace of societal disintegration appears to be accelerating, giving many people the sense that collapse is imminent. Although there are many reasons for concern, three examples will suffice:

1. Our economic prosperity is now a mirage based on unsustainable debt and money creation.

2. The destruction of the family makes social coherency increasingly impossible.

3. A prevailing attitude of entitlement corrupts the desire to be productive and to contribute, thus destroying a significant aspect of what it means to be human.

Seeing the Story Differently

Decline is not inevitable. *With God all things are possible* (Matthew 19:26). He offers to heal our land (2 Chronicles 7:14). The challenge is that we must act. Paul explains the nature of our engagement:

> For though we live in the world, we do not wage war as the world does. The weapons we fight with are not the weapons of the world. On the contrary, they have divine power to demolish strongholds. We demolish arguments and every pretension that sets itself up against the knowledge of God, and we take captive every thought to make it obedient to Christ (2 Corinthians 10:3-5).

The answer to our nation's future is found in grasping the significance of Paul's statement that we currently possess the weapons to demolish "strongholds." We already have at our disposal the resources necessary to demolish "arguments and pretensions" that oppose the knowledge of God. Taking every "thought" captive to the obedience of Christ is well within our present means.

We live in an epic story where the rightful king has invaded earth, beginning a long process of redeeming what was lost. We are not to surrender the world to darkness once again, but rather, we are to commit ourselves to Christ's epic battle to redeem his creation and overcome evil with good.

Winning the War

Although I will often reference Scripture when addressing these issues, I'm not making this case as an academic or theologian, but as the author of the novel *The War Against God*. I am speaking as a fellow traveler who is deeply concerned with the direction of our nation. I believe God is continuously bringing judgment against the City of Man, wherever it is found. We are to rejoice and not despair, for although the expectation of victory is supernaturally reasonable, it will come gradually. Along the way, believers will pass through difficult times of personal suffering, economic hardship and social upheaval.

In the book of Revelation, we are given a picture of what the Lord Jesus is doing from the throne room of heaven as reason for encouragement. Daniel's interpretation of Nebuchadnezzar's dream (Daniel 2) reveals that empires rise and fall in accordance with God's sovereign will. We join the battle with confidence, knowing that our future is guided by the One who governs all human history.

Many of the thoughts and interpretations expressed in *Winning the War* can be traced to the respected biblical scholars and theologians listed in the acknowledgements. Although these Christians have greatly influenced my thinking, none of them is responsible for this work, nor would any of them agree with every point. It is my hope that the reader will find my perspective plausible, Biblically orthodox and latent with redemptive possibility.

To better convey my goals, I draw on introductory remarks from C.S. Lewis to his book on the Psalms:

> This is not a work of scholarship... If an excuse is needed (and perhaps it is) for writing such a book, my excuse would be something like this. It often happens that two schoolboys can solve difficulties in their work for one another better than the master can... The fellow-pupil can help more than the master because he knows less. The difficulty we want him to explain is one he has recently met. The expert met it so long ago that he has forgotten. He sees the whole subject, by now, in such a different light that he cannot conceive what is really troubling the pupil; he sees a dozen other difficulties which ought to be troubling him but aren't.
> In this book, then, I write as one amateur to another, talking about difficulties I have met, or lights I have gained... with the hope that this might at any rate interest, and sometimes even help, other inexpert readers. I am comparing notes, not presuming to instruct.
> ~ C.S. Lewis, *Reflections on the Psalms*

Chapter 1:
Does Our Vision of the Future Matter?

Years ago, a young pastor said to me, "I know what you believe about the growth of God's kingdom, but that's not what I see."

Since becoming a believer more than thirty years ago, I've wrestled with the question of a Christian vision of the future. What is the true reality of the world, who is in control and do the events of our lives have meaning and purpose? While exploring these questions, I became familiar with several different versions of how Christians view the future of the present age. Although Scripture speaks often of what is to come, interpretations vary and consensus proves elusive.

One view, called the "social gospel," proposes to create a better world primarily through political social action based on a somewhat arbitrary determination of the "common good." These social activists tend to rely on the centralized authority of civil government to overcome the reluctance of people to do what the social engineers are convinced is in the society's best interest. I cringe at the thought. Conflating the will of God with centralized authoritarian government is not a proven pathway to a brighter future. History clearly demonstrates that this vision invariably leads, no matter how well intended, to stifling oppression.

Another popular perspective of the future I call "waiting for Jesus" puzzles me, though it is embraced by a majority of evangelical Christians. Although evangelicals are often divided into several theological camps as to the details of what will occur once Jesus returns, they are generally in agreement that until he comes back, Christians and the Church will be on the defensive. They expect evil to continue growing stronger, culminating in the reign of a specific person known as the Antichrist. Any marked manifestation of God's kingdom or significant restraint of evil will have to wait for Jesus to once again physically appear on earth. This popular evangelical vision tends to explain the gospel almost exclusively in terms of personal salvation. Of course, the salvation message is critical – however, does this limited understanding restrict the gospel's intended effect upon the world?

Neither of these commonly held visions of the future appeared to offer much hope for the world. That is why I was intrigued by Matthew Henry's commentary on the Great Commission (Matthew 28:16-18):

> That Christianity should be twisted in with national constitutions, that the kingdoms of the world should become Christ's kingdoms... What is the principal intention of this commission; to disciple all nations... do your utmost to make the nations Christian nations...

> Christ the Mediator is setting up a kingdom in the world, bring the nations to be his subjects...
> ~ Matthew Henry, *Matthew Henry's Commentary on the Whole Bible*[1]

Jonathan Edwards and many believers who lived during the founding of our nation also shared this victorious vision. But few contemporary scholars I encountered seriously considered Matthew Henry's interpretation, so I seldom spoke of this positive view.

Why Our Vision of the Future Matters

My questions about the future returned from an unexpected source – the premature death of my wife of twenty years, the mother of our five children, in 1995. By faith she believed God would heal her from cancer. But he didn't. The problem for me was that I believed God could have. He had healed many before. Yet in this case, he chose not to – why?

I've always believed that God interacts with his created order on a continual basis, that he loves us as a father loves his child. We are not on our own. If he knows the plight of a sparrow, he certainly did

---

[1] Regarding the popularity of Matthew Henry's Commentary on the Whole Bible (1710): Protestant preachers such as George Whitefield and Charles Spurgeon used and heartily commended the work, with Whitefield reading it through four times – the last time on his knees. Spurgeon stated, "Every minister ought to read it entirely and carefully through once at least." Quoted from Wikipedia.

not disregard the supplications of his suffering daughter. Precisely because God's nature is love, I refused to believe that her death was a random mishap. There was too much at stake for it to be a bad break or simply another unfortunate consequence of life in a fallen world. Therefore, I concluded that the answer to the dilemma of her tragic death, or the suffering of any believer in this world, could only be found in God – in his will, his plan, his love for his creation, and his love for a dying mother of five who trusted him with her life and future.

I believed that God, by his very nature, had to be involved. I wasn't sure what that meant exactly, but I will share my feelings at the time of her death. What follows is an excerpt from something I wrote for her memorial service:

> We were soldiers and we had been called into battle. She knew she was to resist with "the weapons of our warfare," and she asked me to fight the battle with her. I struggled to catch up. I did not understand the battle or the price that was paid. But as I stood in her room, I knew she had won. The enemy was scattered and his voice was silenced. She had fought the good fight, she had finished the race and she had most certainly kept the faith.

Faithful Testimony

It wasn't until years later, when considering the story of Job in the light of Revelation 12:11, that I finally understood why her death, in the midst of grief, felt in some ways like a victory:

> They triumphed over him [the devil] by the blood of the Lamb and by the word of their testimony.

What was unveiled to my wounded heart by this verse from Revelation was that just like Job, her suffering and death were not arbitrary. They had been imbued by God with great meaning and purpose. He had enlisted them both as soldiers in his epic battle to overcome evil. **In some small yet significant way that contributes to the ultimate victory, "the enemy was scattered and his voice was silenced" by a dying mother's "faithful testimony."** In the midst of her suffering she trusted God and proclaimed Him "good," the very action the devil tempted Eve, Job and Jesus to not speak.

If this is true, then throughout history all believers are to participate in the ongoing conquest of evil in similar ways. Through the spiritual power of our testimonies, all circumstances – but especially suffering, persecution and tragic death – are redeemed by meaning and purpose. **The cynic is proven wrong. Life is not a cruel hoax, but rather a raging war to defeat evil with good.**

Job's story, when viewed from God's perspective, reveals that the events and circumstances of life, often feeling like combat, set the stage for faithful believers to shine a brilliant light that pierces the very heart of

darkness. As a result, the Kingdom of God continues its rise towards predominance on earth as it is in heaven.

Hope versus Resignation

Theological debates about end-times and the present status of God's kingdom can be challenging and endless. But it may be possible to distill the essence of the arguments into a choice between optimism and pessimism. **Is the resurrection of Christ sufficient to reverse the curse and overcome the effects of Adam's fall? Is the redeeming power of the Gospel sufficient to transform human culture? If the answers are yes, then it is reasonable to expect the victory of the Kingdom of God in time, on earth, prior to Christ's return.**

What does Scripture claim? If Jesus appeared to *destroy the devil's work* (1 John 3:8), and he *disarmed the powers and authorities... triumphing over them* (Colossians 2:15), then we can trust that Satan's kingdom cannot possibly grow stronger in the world (except in specific locations for limited periods of time, i.e., Nazi Germany). If believers are *more than conquerors* (Romans 8:31) and are equipped with *power to demolish strongholds* (2 Corinthians 10:4), if we are instructed to teach all nations *to obey everything I have commanded* (Matthew 28:20) and the gates of hell will not prevail against the Church (Matthew 16:18), then Satan's efforts to dominate the present age and suppress God's people will prove futile – **unless God's people enable Satan's success by not exercising Christ's authority**.

The young pastor I encountered had a vision of the future that was determined by what he observed. But are we to trust our sight? Similar to the ten spies in the Promised Land, our eyes may convince us that against the forces of darkness we are *like grasshoppers* (Numbers 13:33). Perhaps, like Joshua and Caleb, we should listen to what the Spirit tells us.

Chapter 2.
God Starts With the End in Mind

> Known unto God are all his works from the beginning of the world (Acts 15:18).

When trying to understand the present state of the world, our nation, or even our own lives, we tend to look to the past. Although history does provide some insight, it cannot adequately explain present circumstances. The true meaning of events can only be found in God's purpose for the future. Scripture assures us that our experiences on earth, both the good and the evil, are not random acts. God oversees what he conceived from the very beginning. Fortunately for humanity, this includes his desire to create eternal sons and daughters who will live in relationship with the Trinity forever.

History is the revelation of his eternal plan as it unfolds in time and space. Due to God's omniscience (or more specifically, his foreknowledge), **we can be confident that the world we live in exists as always intended by God to best suite his purposes. If there had been a better way for him to achieve his desired results, then we would be living in that story instead of this one. Anything different than what is, would have resulted in something less than what God desires. The Father's nature ensures that the plan was conceived in love. Therefore, we trust God and his plan because we know he is good, no matter how things may appear from our shortsighted perspective.**

His hand guides this story. Thus, the events of our lives, of all history, have significance as scenes advancing his purposes. This perspective leads to a peculiar realization: the past does not determine our future. We have been set free from what was, so that we can become what we are to be – a new creation. That is why we are to forget what is behind (Philippians 3:13) and press onward. **We are no more intended to remain a creature of the dust than a butterfly is to remain a caterpillar.**

In the mystery of God's redemption of the world and his plan to see it accomplished, what is to happen in the future unveils the meaning of the present and the past. Our responsibility is to trust in the good outcome promised to us:

> And we know that all things work together for good to those who love God, to those who are called according to His purpose. (Romans 8:28)

Chapter 3:
Why Would God Allow Evil to Enter His Creation?

> [It is] more befitting His power and goodness to bring good out of evil than to prevent the evil from coming into existence...
> ~ St. Augustine, *The City of God*

In the beginning, God gave Adam and Eve free will, creative imagination, and a reasoning intellect that enabled them to love and to be truly relational. These qualities led Adam and Eve to explore the possibilities, push the limits and question God's intent, which led to disobedience and sin.

The operation of free will and the practice of a right relationship with God could not be maintained unless Adam and Eve willingly surrendered their desire to choose to sin. Yet they could not know or imagine exactly what they would be surrendering or why. They lacked a context for understanding why they should restrain their creative imaginations because they possessed no prior knowledge of the consequences. **They would have to experience for themselves how sin corrupts what is good and beautiful, what it means to be miserable, and the pain of separation caused by death.**

Now, having experienced evil, both personally and historically, believers enter the Kingdom of God conscious of the consequences of sin, not as fleeting emotional angst, but as knowledge embedded in our memories forever.

The misery of evil also animates our search for the source of truth, beauty and goodness. We discover these attributes in God when we return to him, and like the father of the prodigal son, he greets us with open arms. Our spirit renounces its rebellion; we accept his love and embrace his care. We feel as though we have returned home when we surrender with peace of heart and mind. We allow God to restore our true nature, enabling Christ to bring forth our truest selves.

Our voluntary surrender, prompted by a flight from the misery of evil, gives God permission to write his law upon our hearts and to indwell us with the Holy Spirit who empowers, protects and guides us through life and eternity. We are now raised from the spiritually dead, born again, experiencing the first resurrection (Ephesians 2:5-6, Colossians 2:12-13). We have become God's new creations: "Therefore, if anyone is in Christ, he is a new creation. The old has passed away; behold, the new has come" (2 Corinthians 5:17, RSV).

God allowed Satan to enter the Garden of Eden. God's plan to bring good out of evil was set in motion by Adam and Eve's response to the serpent's deceit. **Through an ongoing process of redemption, God has been transforming his creatures of dust into "new creations," the sons and daughters with whom he will share eternity.**

God's sovereignty leads us to believe that his "new creations" must have been his objective from the very beginning. This insight helps to explain the story we live in. God creates a man in his image whose rebellion is catalyzed by an agent of evil. To overcome the consequences of rebellion, the man voluntarily surrenders his desire to be his own god. By surrendering, the creature of dust gives the Father permission to transform him into the likeness of his Son. When Satan and the powers of evil no longer serve God's purpose, they will be eliminated. **It is critical to understanding history, the future, and the Christian life. Evil will eventually be destroyed and victory achieved by Jesus through the participation of his "new creation" people.**

Chapter 4:
What If Jesus Had All Authority?

And though this world, with devils filled,
should threaten to undo us; we will not fear,
for God hath willed his truth to triumph
through us.
~ Martin Luther, *A Mighty Fortress is Our God*

Are Satan and his forces of evil the power currently reigning on earth? Is he on the offensive or is he desperately trying to defend his turf?

As the master of deception, Satan's primary deceit is that he is the indomitable power of this age. There was a time when Satan could offer Jesus the kingdoms of this world, but that ended 2,000 years ago. In the shadow of the crucifixion, Jesus said, "Now the prince of this world will be driven out" (John 12:31). Paul later commented, "And having disarmed the powers and authorities, he made a public spectacle of them, triumphing over them by the cross" (Colossians. 2:15).

The apostle John reported more extensively on Satan's present circumstances in Revelation 20:1-3.

> I saw an angel coming down out of heaven,
> having the key to the Abyss and holding in his
> hand a great chain. He seized the dragon, that
> ancient serpent... and bound him for a
> thousand years... to keep him from deceiving
> the nations anymore until the thousand years
> were ended.

In the book of Revelation, numbers are primarily symbolic. "A thousand years" means a very long time and refers to the present age between the first advent of Christ and his Second Coming. (See Appendix A.)

Although we have been informed that Satan has been "bound," we cannot be sure what it means to bind a spiritual being. What we do know is that Satan's power has been significantly restrained, "to keep him from deceiving the nations," even though he is still "like a roaring lion looking for someone to devour" (1 Peter 5:8).

Yet if God's kingdom is at hand and the devil's power is limited, why do so many believers seem willing to accept Satan's narrative that Jesus did not intend "thy will be done on earth as it is in heaven" for the age into which it was spoken? We have too quickly accepted that the fulfillment of the Great Commission means something substantially less than the actual discipleship of all nations. Did Jesus not promise to build his Church, which the gates of Hell cannot overcome? Did he not give us power to tread on the enemy?

Many Christians believe that the Kingdom of God on earth, in this present age, is no match for Satan, the world's Caesars, or its enlightened humanists and mockers. Many visualize earth as a holding tank in which they await the opportunity to retreat to another world. They insist that God's kingdom will not be manifest on earth until Jesus physically returns. This view is reminiscent of Peter's failure after briefly walking on the water. Like Peter, after some initial success (from twelve disciples to hundreds of millions of believers), Christians often look at the condition of the world around them, lose heart and begin to sink:

> "Lord, if it is you," Peter replied, "tell me to come to you on the water."
> "Come," he said.
> Then Peter got down out of the boat, walked on the water and came toward Jesus. But when he saw the wind, he was afraid and, beginning to sink, cried out, "Lord, save me!"
> Immediately Jesus reached out his hand and caught him. (Matthew 14:29-31a)

Was Peter congratulated for his humility and faith when he cried out for Jesus to rescue him from the danger surrounding him? No, not at all. Jesus wasted no time chastising Peter:

> "You of little faith, why did you doubt?" (Matthew 14:31b)

The Nature of Authority and Faith

By way of contrast, consider the one of whom Jesus said, "I tell you the truth, I have not found anyone in Israel with such *great faith*" (Luke 7:9). Of whom was Jesus speaking? One of his disciples? A follower of John the Baptist? A Jewish religious leader?

No, ironically, he was talking about a centurion, a Roman military officer. And what was the evidence of this *great faith*? **He believed Jesus did not need**

to be physically present to accomplish what he intended. Jesus only needed to give the command, to "But say the word" and the centurion's servant would be healed (Luke 7:7). The centurion understood that Jesus had authority sufficient to guarantee the completion of the task. Such is the nature of authority, and such is the nature of faith.

Once Jesus told Peter to come across the water, Peter only needed to get out of the boat and walk. He failed when he began to doubt Jesus' authority, an authority and power that Jesus had repeatedly demonstrated could transcend all circumstances. **Where Jesus happened to be was inconsequential to his ability to accomplish his purposes.**

Again, it is important to note that Jesus did not make this incredible statement about the centurion's great faith because the centurion believed Jesus could heal his servant. Many people had faith that Jesus could heal. But the remarkable statement from Jesus was due to the centurion's understanding that "authority" over the physical world was the source of Jesus' power. In other words, healing was not something Jesus performed as much as it was something he commanded.

Jesus did not make the water into wine, but rather he commanded the molecular structure of the water to change. **This is why Jesus does not need to be present in order to usher in his kingdom. Anything he wishes to accomplish on earth can be achieved from the throne room of heaven.**

This is the significance of the centurion's understanding.

Christ is the:

> Alpha and omega; far above all rule and authority, power and dominion... in the present age; making all things new; disarming the powers and authorities; the ruler of the kings of the earth; in whose name the nations put their hope (Revelation 1:8, Ephesians 1:21, Revelation 21:5, Colossians 2:15, Revelation 1:5, Matthew 12:21).

These powerful claims of scripture give us sufficient reason to question any view of the future that envisions an oppressed, powerless Church that must be rescued by the physical return of Jesus. To the contrary, God's word requires his *will be done on* [this present] *earth as in heaven*. With all authority and power, Jesus directs us to "make disciples of all nations... teaching them to obey everything I have commanded." Paul adds, "If God is for us, who can be against us?... In all these things we are more than conquerors through him who loved us" (Romans 8:31, 37).

These are not words of retreat or feel-good sentiments with no practical application in reality. They are marching orders for Christ's people in this present age. **The world is at war. The powers and principalities of darkness are challenging Christ's authority through the City of Man. Therefore, this world is where the battle must be fought and won.**

Jesus will remain in the heavenly realm until he has defeated his enemies (1 Corinthians 15:25). He will come back after he has won the victory, not in order to win it. After all, would the Trinity really devise a plan from before time began in which Christ's authority on earth and the presence of the Holy Spirit would be insufficient to save our Father's world and destroy the spiritual power of evil? Did Jesus pray for our unity and abiding strength only for us to be divided, dissipated and weak? Until these this questions are answered, life on earth will remain a perplexing mystery.

Chapter 5:
Continual Spiritual Warfare: Dispossessing the City of Man

In Revelation chapters 4-6, we are invited into heaven through the experience of the disciple John. Much to our surprise, John does not describe a pastoral scene with the Good Shepherd, the saints, and our deceased loved ones enjoying peaceful, angelic harp interludes. **He leads us into the very throne room of God where we witness the fervent activity of a central command headquarters.**

Flashes of lightning. Rumblings and peals of thunder. The prayers of God's people rising as incense before the throne. "Standing in the center of the throne," encircled by creatures, elders, and throngs of angels, is "the Lion of the tribe of Judah… a Lamb looking as if it had been slain" (Revelation 5:5-6).

John recognizes Jesus Christ, the true heir of David, the promised king worshipped by shepherds and wise men, welcomed by the *whole world* (John 12:19) when he entered Jerusalem to claim his rightful throne. But he was rejected and killed by the wayward stewards of temple and empire.

An explanation of what we are witnessing in Revelation 6 is found in the Parable of the Tenants (Matthew 21:33-39) where Jesus said:

> "A landowner planted a vineyard and rented it to some farmers. After the harvest, he sent

his servants to collect his fruit. The tenants seized the servants; they beat one, killed another, and stoned a third... Last of all, he sent his son to them... **But when the tenants saw the son, they said to each other, 'This is the heir. Come, let's kill him and take his inheritance.'** So they took him and threw him out of the vineyard and killed him."

When the chief priests and the Pharisees heard Jesus' parables, **they knew he was talking about them.**

Just as in the parable, Jesus was confronted by false stewards who refused to acknowledge the true heir. Jesus revealed in the parable that the chief priests and Pharisees knew he was the "son," the rightful ruler who had come to repossess what had been lost. But they had no intention of relinquishing their control.

The Old Testament foreshadowed this event. Moses confronted Pharaoh who refused to release God's people from Egyptian captivity. About forty years later, Joshua crossed the Jordan to drive out the Canaanites who would not surrender the land God had given to Abraham, Isaac and Jacob. Then, over a thousand years later, shortly after Christ's ascension, John recorded in his vision from the command center of heaven that one greater than Moses or Joshua, the Lord Jesus Christ, opened the seals and initiated judgment against those who opposed his reign. The great shaking of the world during the present kingdom age had begun (Revelation 6).

A Conqueror Bent on Conquest

John saw the Lord Jesus. *Before me was a white horse. Its rider held a bow, and he was given a crown, and he rode out as a conqueror bent on conquest* (Revelation 6:2). Jesus was leading the charge across a mystical Jordan River into the new worldwide Canaan, what St. Augustine famously called "the City of Man." There was to be no geographical limitation: *Go and make disciples of all nations"* (Matthew 28:17). *Go into all the world* (Mark 16:15). Theologian Abraham Kuyper summarized this thought well:

> There is not a square inch in the whole domain of our human existence over which Christ, who is Sovereign over all, does not cry, Mine!

Behind Jesus follows the wrath of God just as it had followed Moses into Egypt and Joshua into the Promised Land. Yet similar to Pharaoh's refusal to release God's people from slavery and the Canaanites determination to maintain possession of the Promised Land, so also the City of Man has arrogantly dismissed any claim Jesus has on the world and its people.

After the Flood, the rebellious spirit of man prompted the construction of a great tower on the plains of Shinar in defiance of God. "Then they said, 'Come, let us build ourselves a city, with a tower that reaches to the heavens, so that we can make a name for ourselves'" (Genesis 11:4). These proud men, united in opposition to God, proclaimed their intention to take their future into their own hands and dominate creation to their own ends. Although God frustrated their original effort by confusing their languages, men have not abandoned their determination to establish a man-centered world order that is free from what they perceive to be the tyranny and foolishness of a barbaric deity. Nevertheless, God takes their actions seriously; for he says in reference to the Tower of Babel that if men succeed, "Then nothing they plan to do will be impossible for them" (Genesis 11:6).

No matter what form the Tower of Babel has taken (the Roman Empire, the Communist Workers Paradise, the Nazi's Thousand Year Reich, or any other statist utopian dream), God has continued to thwart man's efforts. But the objectives of rebellious humanity remain the same, and the battle still rages. The City of Man enlists anyone and everyone who is not securely in God's kingdom into its war against the co-heirs of Christ.

Besides their pretension to be lords of the earth, the City of Man also attempts to infiltrate the true Church. Claiming enlightened wisdom, false prophets advance an alliance with corrupt, oppressive government schemes that profess to provide humanity's every need.

Throughout history, the City of Man has fought to prevent the manifestation of Christ's kingdom. Yet Revelation reveals that Jesus is currently procuring the victory – protecting the eternal souls of believers, purifying his Church and bearing judgment from the heavenly realms upon those in rebellion against his throne.

Chapter 6:
Satan Empowers the City of Man

> For our struggle is not against flesh and blood, but against the rulers, against the authorities, against the powers of this dark world and against the spiritual forces of evil in the heavenly realms (Ephesians. 6:12).

As the spiritual dimensions of heaven's ongoing war against the rebellious City of Man become clear, our understanding of life and history deepens. In Revelation 12 and 13, John describes the scope and nature of this epic conflict.

> The great dragon…that ancient serpent called the devil, or Satan, who leads the whole world astray… was enraged at the woman and went off to make war against the rest of her offspring – those who obey God's commandments and hold to the testimony of Jesus. And the dragon stood on the shore of the sea. And I saw a beast coming out of the sea. He had ten horns and seven heads, with ten crowns on his horns…. The dragon gave the beast his power and his throne and great authority.

Revelation can be frustrating when one attempts to impose a chronological order and ascribe specific persons or places to metaphoric symbols. The meaning of John's vision opens up when one interprets the symbolism in the light of a cosmic struggle that began with the birth of Jesus in

Bethlehem and will continue until the Second Coming and the consummation of all things.

In regard to the specific symbolism of Revelation 12 and 13, the great dragon is Satan. The woman and her offspring represent the true Church, throughout history. The beast rising out of the sea (the unbelieving world) had 7 heads and 10 horns with 10 crowns. Perhaps John imagined the Roman empire of his day when he first viewed the beast. But because the numbers (7 and 10) symbolize fullness and totality, we are prompted to look out across all of history at man's unrelenting quest for empire. In this light, we realize that the beast does not need to be confined to a particular time or place, but rather symbolizes all human government and culture apart from God, and the pursuit of power and empire throughout all ages, past and future. (See Appendix A.)

A significant aspect of Satan's strategy is revealed in Revelation 13. Quite possibly due to the restraints imposed on him, and his present inability to directly deceive the nations (Revelations 20:2-3), Satan has chosen to align the powers of spiritual darkness with the City of Man. He empowers a humanistic culture determined to create a new, Christless paradise on earth. **Into the image of the beast, with cruelty and malice, Satan pours** *his power and his throne and great authority* **(Revelation 13:2). In other words, the enemies of God have concentrated their spiritual power against Christ and his Church into human government and culture.**

John then describes a second beast as coming out of the earth in Revelation 12:11-13.

> He had two horns like a lamb, but he spoke like a dragon. He exercised all the authority of the first beast on his behalf, and made the earth and its inhabitants worship the first beast.

This second beast symbolizes religious power in the service of the governing authorities of the City of Man. It is the false church that offers a salvation found in secular culture and social action. **It advances a humanistic unity, a desire to make all faiths one, ultimately worshipping a deified state as the pinnacle of human community.** Its goals require a collective consciousness enforced by conformity to the social, political and economic goals of the ruling philosopher-kings. To its converts, it promises the protection and blessings of the state – the mark of the beast.

We Are Soldiers in the Battle

As co-heirs with Christ, we are beginning to realize that an epic war of kingdoms is being waged on earth. What comes as a shock to many believers is the suggestion that **we, the body of Christ, are not just the focal point of the enemy's hostility. We are also expected to be soldiers in the battle.**

The Lord Jesus commands his armies from the throne of heaven. Throughout the age, as described in Revelation, his angels administer three sets of seven judgments upon the City of Man. The souls of the elect are protected. The serpent's delusions are embraced by the unbelieving world, resulting in a self-destructive irrationality. Autonomous man is a rebel, making social coherency impossible. That is why humanism must seek power to enforce its utopian dreams. **But the common good that it allegedly pursues is inevitably crushed by the coercive force used to achieve it.**

As the Lord scatters his foes during the course of the battle, it is the duty of his soldiers on the ground to occupy the territory he has won. The role of individual Christians might be better understood by using a metaphor: foot soldiers during World War II.

Historians could say that the defeat of Nazi Germany was inevitable the moment the United States joined the conflict. But the actual war still had to be fought by soldiers in historical time and space. The foot soldiers did not arm themselves, nor determine their own theater of operation, nor draw up specific battle plans. But the victory was dependent on the soldiers faithfully carrying out their orders to "demolish enemy strongholds" and "set the captives free."

Soldiers were expected to confront the enemy, sometimes hand-to-hand. They often faced insurmountable odds; it was not uncommon for them to feel overwhelmed. Yet they were not to lose hope even when threatened with death, always trusting that the means of victory, though out of sight, was continuously flowing to the front lines. The soldiers knew there would be fierce resistance, lost skirmishes and surrendered gains at times. Death and suffering would be experienced. But from the perspective of the command center, foot soldiers occupying territory was a necessary phase for the inevitable total victory.

Babylon – The Utopian Dream

The Apostle John's vision in Revelation offers an overarching description of the spiritual dimensions of the conflict with evil engulfing our world. A critical example is the spiritual concept embodied by the Tower of Babel. It was not just a place or city; it was an idea that captivated the fallen world of man. The dream of a united social order under a one world government later found expression in the ancient empire of Babylon. That empire was eventually conquered, but the Bible continued to use the name Babylon, which in Hebrew is also Babel, as a representation of the world system opposed to God's authority.

In Revelation 12 and 13, as previously discussed, John observed two beasts. The first is the embodiment of all humanistic governments and cultures. The second beast is the false church, leading all faiths to unite in the worship of the first beast. Later an angel shows John "a woman sitting on a scarlet beast that was covered with blasphemous names and had seven heads and ten horns" (Revelation 17:3). The woman that rides the first beast is more than a ruler, or empire, or false prophet. She is rebellious man's ultimate ideal – for by her *magic spell all the nations were led astray*

(Revelation 18:23). She is the utopian dream of an earthly paradise without God. She is *Babylon*.

> Babylon the Great… the great prostitute, who sits on many waters (peoples, multitudes, nations, and languages)… with her the kings of the earth committed adultery and the inhabitants of the earth were intoxicated with the wine of her adulteries…. The woman you saw is the great city that rules over the kings of the earth (Revelation 17).

Babylon is more than a person or place because *she* personifies the entire world system in rebellion against God. The spirit of Babylon promises power and empire, wealth and progress by human legislation, and freedom from guilt and sin. Revelation 17 reveals a picture of the world system embraced by humanistic governments and cultures that are *seduced* by the promise of an earthly paradise and *intoxicated* by the power to achieve it. John's account warns believers not to be co-opted by Babylon's seductive dreams or to take them lightly. Challenging their imagined future of a one world government and social order provokes their wrath.

> I saw the woman was drunk with the blood of the saints, the blood of those who bore testimony to Jesus (Revelation 17:6).

For the Church's benefit, the angel revealed to John that the ideas driving the world system, what Revelation calls the spirit of Babylon, are empowered by spiritual darkness. We are to expect the battle, and be prepared for it. We are to abide in Christ, united for strength.

Chapter 7:
Babylon Falls

> Fallen! Fallen is Babylon the Great! She has become a home for demons and a haunt for every evil spirit (Revelation 18:2).

Since his ascension to the throne, Jesus, the rightful king, has issued forth judgments upon the City of Man. His goals are first to purify his bride – breaking the spell of Babylon as he calls his people out of the world system and sets them free to worship the Lord and live in the power of the Holy Spirit. Secondly, he is dislodging the false stewards as he builds his kingdom so that His will is done *on earth as it is in heaven* (Matthew 6:10).

As John describes events from the throne room of heaven, we realize that walking by sight will leave us in the dark. The more one tries to decipher John's vision by observing specific current events, the more fanciful and improbable the interpretations become. John's vision is easier to understand when it is seen as a description of an ongoing cosmic war with good overcoming evil throughout our present age.

To further understand John's vision, we should avoid the assumption that descriptions are linear and specific. (After all, the kingdom of the world became the kingdom of our Lord and of his Christ in chapter 11, and Christ was born in chapter 12.) Revelation is not about zeroing in on future predictions, but encouraging the Church by describing the overarching story – **that Jesus is gradually permeating a corrupted world with the**

true spiritual reality of his kingdom (Matthew 13:33).

Revelation also tells us that judgment has fallen, is falling, and will fall on Babylon throughout history. Did not the rulers and merchants of Rome, and the Ottoman Empire, and the Third Reich *weep and mourn over her?* What about the rulers and merchants of all the former kingdoms of man? Did they not weep and mourn when her promises proved illusory? Will future rulers and merchants of a Progressive socialist new world order or an Islamic caliphate not weep and mourn when their dreams of power, wealth and paradise are *brought to ruin?* (Revelation 18:19)

> Woe! Woe, O great city, O Babylon, city of power! ... Her plagues will overtake her; death, mourning and famine. She will be consumed by fire, for mighty is the Lord God who judges her (Revelation 18:8, 10).

Breaking Babylon's Spell

Despite this promise of judgment, the magic spell of Babylon still pervades the world. Her promises remain seductive. Revelation 18 starts with an angel descending, illuminating the earth. The angel's words impart understanding. Some have come to see the deceptions of the world system, but many others remain naïve or deceived. When considering the admonition that follows, we glimpse why God may be patiently withholding his final judgment of Babylon.

> I heard another voice from heaven say,
> "Come out of her, my people, so that you will

not share in her sins, so that you will not
receive any of her plagues" (Revelation 18:4).

By "come out of her," the Lord does not intend for us to turn the church into a fortress so we can withdraw from the world. We are not to be *of the world* [the world system], but we are to be salt and light *in the world* [God's good creation]. We are to be active agents of cultural renewal, recognizing that there is no neutral ground in the conflict. There is no sacred/secular divide. We are to carry the good news of Christ's kingdom into a hostile world, demolishing strongholds by taking every thought captive to the obedience of Christ – which includes not just our personal lives, but every thought about government, economics, education, science and health, media and the arts, and all areas of life.

Even the rulers and merchants will eventually hate the world system, for it cannot fulfill their dreams. Their self-idolatry will compel greed and corruption, perverting, and thus destroying, any possible fulfillment of their earthly paradise. Therefore, "they will bring her to ruin and leave her naked; and eat her flesh and burn her with fire." When they look upon "the smoke of her burning," a blaze they will have brought upon themselves, "they will weep and mourn over her" (Revelation 18).

These judgments of heaven upon the City of Man have been, and will continue to be, difficult to live through for everyone, including Christians. So how should we, the body of Christ on earth, respond to our Lord's war against the rebellious stewards when it affects our lives, our families and the communities where we live?

Revelation prescribes a clear response to God's judgment of Babylon. "Rejoice over her, O heaven! Rejoice, saints and apostles and prophets! God has judged her for the way she treated you" (Revelation 18:20).

The answer is *rejoice,* even though rejoicing may prove difficult when it might be our own nation falling under judgment. **But the shaking is essential, preparing both believers and the world for the continuing advance of Christ's kingdom on the earth.** Babylon's influence is destined to end, "never to be found again." Her judgment is set, for she is guilty. "In her was found the blood... of all who have been killed on the earth" (Revelation 18:24).

The devastation of Babylon will affect nations and communities – economic hardship and breakdowns of social order will ensue. **But out of the ever-churning turbulence of the world's chaos, Christ's kingdom will rise victorious. The way is being cleared for the fulfillment of the Great Commission and the kingdom promises.** With purpose determined before the beginning of time, we once again see Jesus on a white horse, riding from heaven across the world's stage.

> With justice he judges and makes war....
> And his name is the Word of God.... Out of his mouth comes a sharp sword with which to strike down the nations.... On his robe and his thigh he has this name written: King of kings and Lord of lords (Revelation 19:11-16).

Chapter 8:
Christ's Kingdom Rises

> For unto us a child is born.... Of the greatness of his government and peace there will be no end. He will reign on David's throne ... establishing and upholding it with justice and righteousness **from that time on** and forever. **The zeal of the Lord Almighty will accomplish this** (Isaiah 9:6-7).

Seven hundred years after this prophecy from Isaiah, Jesus began his ministry. He announced to the world, "I must preach the good news of the kingdom of God... because that is why I was sent" (Luke 4:43). As Jesus shared insights into God's kingdom, he immediately ran into an entrenched resistance – the Jewish expectation of a political, messianic kingdom. The author of the best-selling novel, *Ben-Hur*, captured this expectation:

> The unanimity among the chosen people was a matter of marvelous astonishment: the messiah was to be, when come, the King of the Jews – their political King, their Caesar. By their instrumentality he was to make armed conquest of the earth, and then, for their profit and in the name of God, hold it down forever.
> ~ Lew Wallace, *Ben-Hur: A Tale of the Christ*

Once those entrenched in power in Jerusalem realized that Jesus had not come to serve their interests, they crucified him. Yet the story did not end. Jesus was not only raised from the dead, but he ascended to the right hand of the Father just as prophesied 1,000 years earlier by King David. "The Lord says to my Lord: 'Sit at my right hand until I make your enemies a footstool for your feet'" (Psalm 110).

After the resurrection, the disciples saw Jesus "ascend into the clouds" (Acts 1:9). But equally intriguing was Daniel's vision that took place six centuries before, when Daniel prophetically witnessed Christ's ascension from the vantage point of heaven, as Jesus came up to the Father.

> In my vision at night I looked, and there before me was one like a son of man, coming with the clouds of heaven. He approached the Ancient of Days and was led into his presence. He was given authority, glory and sovereign power: all peoples, nations and men of every language worshiped him. His dominion is an everlasting dominion that will not pass away, and his kingdom is one that will never be destroyed (Daniel 7:13-14).

In other words, Jesus Christ ascended into heaven, to his throne, to his command center, in order to rule the earth with all authority, glory and sovereign power *until* his will *is* done, "on earth as it is in heaven" (Matthew 6:10).

To empower his people to manifest his will on earth, Jesus was "exalted to the right hand of God, he has received from the Father the promised Holy Spirit and has poured out what you now see and hear" (Acts 2:32-33). At Pentecost, a small group of believers received "power from on high" (Luke 24:49), transforming them from cowards into spiritual warriors. Thus was launched God's strategy for the transformation of the world – the Great Commission – given by Jesus to his disciples. "**All authority** in heaven and **on earth** has been given to me. Therefore go and make disciples of **all nations**... teaching them to obey everything I have commanded you" (Matthew 28:18-20).

Many years later, the apostle John was on the island of Patmos. Although we are not told what John was thinking, we can imagine what would have been weighing on his mind as he contemplated the kingdom's progress. John knew that Satan had been defeated by the cross and the resurrection. Paul had even written "The God of peace will soon crush Satan under your feet" (Romans 16:20). Nevertheless, it was obvious that the devil still exercised much influence in the world. Paul and some of the other disciples were probably martyred by this time. The new churches were suffering persecution throughout the Roman Empire. The temple in Jerusalem had either been destroyed or was about to be.

I imagine John sometimes felt alone and, in his worst moments, even a little depressed. He must have carried deep concerns for the early Church. Apostasy was on the rise. Many believers were questioning the true gospel. The fulfillment of the Great Commission seemed further away than ever. Perhaps doubts were beginning to surface.

It would not be surprising if John, while watching wisps of white clouds drift above the peaceful Mediterranean Sea, with the sound of waves lapping upon the shore, had wondered what Jesus, his friend and lord, was doing at that moment. What was the plan? Was Jesus depending on them to do something? John might have thought of Elisha asking God to reveal to his servant the spiritual reality surrounding them. "Then the Lord opened the servant's eyes, and he looked and saw the hills full of horses and chariots of fire" (2 Kings 6:15-17). It might have been at just a moment like this when John heard a loud voice:

> I turned around to see the voice that was speaking to me.... His face was like the sun shining in all its brilliance. When I saw him, I fell at his feet as though dead. Then he placed his right hand on me and said, "Do not be afraid.... Write... what you have seen, what is now and what will take place later" (Revelation 1:12, 16-19).

After the experience of Revelation, John's heart must have been overwhelmed with joy. The kingdom was advancing, directed from the throne room of heaven. Jesus was actively bringing about the victory in his time and in his way. Yet all believers by their faithful actions and prayers were participating. Of course the Great Commission will be fulfilled. All power and authority will prove to mean *all*, as the nations become disciples of Christ, obeying his teaching. The kingdom promises of Isaiah and others will be fulfilled.

Chapter 8: Christ's Kingdom Rises

The Gradual Growth of God's Kingdom

Jesus taught that the Kingdom of heaven was like a mustard seed.

> The smallest of all your seeds, yet when it grows, it is the largest of garden plants and becomes a tree. Or it is like yeast that a woman took and mixed into a large amount of flour until it worked all through the dough (Matthew 13:31-33).

Jesus had described the advance of his kingdom as a gradual progression – **from inauspicious beginnings to total predominance.** A similar view was offered by Daniel when he interpreted Nebuchadnezzar's dream. After describing the four earthly kingdoms of the enormous statue (Babylon, Medo-Persian, Greece and Rome), Daniel continued.

> A rock was cut out, but not by human hands. It struck the statue on its feet of iron and clay and smashed them.... The wind swept them away without leaving a trace. **But the rock that struck the statue became a huge mountain and filled the whole earth....** *In the time of those kings*, **the God of heaven will set up a Kingdom that will never be destroyed** (Daniel 2:34, 35, 44).

Daniel's vision of the rock that becomes a huge mountain echoes Isaiah's prophecy concerning the kingdom as it grows into predominance between the first coming of Christ and his second coming. It is the time period Isaiah refers to as the "last days" and which Peter defines at Pentecost (Acts 2:16-17). (See Appendix A.)

> Now it will come about that in the last days the mountain of the house of the Lord will be established as the chief of the mountains, and will be raised above the hills; and all the nations will stream to it. And many peoples will come and say, "Come, let us go up to the mountain of the Lord, to the house of the God of Jacob; that He may teach us concerning **His ways** and that we may walk in **His paths**" (Isaiah 2:2-3 NASB).

Isaiah tells us that during the present age, between the first and second comings of Christ, "the Lord's mountain will be raised above the hills" in order to be "established as the chief of the mountains." This compares to Daniel's rock that "became a huge mountain and filled the whole earth."

Isaiah and Daniel's description of God's advancing kingdom as a "growing mountain" is a metaphor repeated in the New Testament as the symbolic Mount Zion described in Hebrews. "You have not come to a mountain that can be touched…. But you have come to Mount Zion, to the heavenly Jerusalem, the city of the living God… to the church of the first born" (Hebrews 12:18, 22-23).

Isaiah's prophecy and the Great Commission describe the same future for the world – all the nations of the earth will come to the new Mount Zion, "the church of the first born," to seek God's wisdom and direction for every area of life, because there is nowhere in human experience and culture where "his ways" and "his paths" do not govern. That is why we are to take every thought captive to the obedience of Christ.

The same pattern of insignificance to predominance was again evident in Ezekiel's vision of the unusual river flowing from a new temple. The depth of the water coming out from under the threshold was only ankle-deep. Yet the farther Ezekiel moved from the source of the stream, the deeper it became, until "it was deep enough to swim in – a river no one could cross" (Ezekiel 47:5). From the Father's right hand, Jesus, the true temple, is pouring out the Holy Spirit so that for whoever believes "streams of living water will flow from within him" (John 7:38). Ezekiel's vision represents the Holy Spirit's increasing influence over the course of this present age.

Restoring Our Created Image

A primary purpose of the kingdom is the ongoing restoration of the image of God in human beings. Initiated by a voluntary act of surrender prompted by the Holy Spirit (repentance), individuals begin a process of supernatural internal transformation. The outward expression of this internal change, especially when conscientiously practiced with other believers, will have a transformational effect on communities and cultures. As a consequence of our heart-felt love for the Lord, we desire to obey him and to faithfully reign with him over whatever we find within our personal domains.

The kingdom's growth mirrors the individual's growth phases of salvation, sanctification and resurrection. At the ascension, Jesus was crowned king and he now rules. The world is going through a sanctification process as Jesus continues to plunder lost souls from Satan's kingdom. He is making all things new, starting with believers, his "new creations" (2 Corinthians 5:16-18), who are entering the "new Jerusalem" (Hebrews 12:22).

Over the course of history, the change from insignificance to predominance will become increasingly evident. Babylon's spell will be broken. Great numbers will "come out of" and reject, to a substantial degree, the world system's counterfeit promises.

The spiritual reality of Christ's reign will increasingly affect the quality of life on earth. The mustard plant's leaves will extend above the other garden plants. The rock in Daniel's vision will rise above the surrounding hills to become Isaiah's "chief of the mountains." Even those who do not embrace Christ's rule will nevertheless benefit as self-destructive tendencies are tempered due to the influence and loving care of common grace.

The promise to Abraham will come clearly into view that "all peoples on earth will be blessed through you" (Genesis 12:3) as the healing qualities of the rising kingdom gradually bring "restoration to all of creation" (Romans 8:21-22). **The anticipated blessings of the manifestation of God's kingdom in this present age, announced by the prophets, will impart peace, prosperity and**

healing to the nations, to both Christians and non-believers alike, as when a gentle rain blesses both the wheat and the tares.

We can be grateful that the Lord Jesus reigns for his purpose. "God did not send his Son into the world to condemn the world, but to save the world through him" (John 3:17). By faith we believe that saving the world is what he's actively doing. As a result, the kingdom prophecies of Isaiah and others will come to pass.

> Never again will there be in it an infant who lives but a few days, or an old man who does not live out his years; **he who dies at a hundred will be thought a mere youth**; he who fails to reach a hundred will be considered accursed (Isaiah 65:20).

> Everyone will sit under their own vine and under their own fig tree, **and no one will make them afraid**, for the Lord Almighty has spoken (Micah 4:4).

> No longer will they build houses and others live in them, or plant and others eat... My chosen ones will long enjoy the work of their hands. **They will not labor in vain, nor will they bear children doomed to misfortune**; for they will be a people blessed by the Lord, they and their descendants with them. Before they call I will answer; while they are still speaking I will hear (Isaiah 65:22-24).

> He will judge between the nations and will settle disputes for many peoples. They will beat their swords into plowshares and their spears into pruning hooks. **Nation will not take up sword against nation, nor will they train for war anymore** (Isaiah 2:4).

> "I will put my law in their minds and write it on their hearts. I will be their God, and they will be my people. **No longer will they teach their neighbor, or say to one another, 'Know the Lord,' because they will all know me,** from the least of them to the greatest," declares the Lord (Jeremiah 31:33-34).

In chapter 11, Isaiah could be speaking of a partial restoration of the original harmony of nature, or he could be speaking symbolically of changes that come over individuals and people groups who no longer fit the description of wild beasts. Maybe he means both, wherever appropriate. What is important is that the growing kingdom changes the very nature of men and beasts.

> The wolf will live with the lamb, the leopard will lie down with the goat... and the lion will eat straw like the ox. The infant will play near the cobra's den, and the young child will put its hand into the viper's nest. They will neither harm nor destroy on all my holy mountain, **for the earth will be filled with the knowledge of the Lord** as the waters cover the sea (Isaiah 11:6-9).

Dallas Willard said, "A time will come in human history when human beings will follow the Ten Commandments and so on as regularly as they now fall to the ground when they step off a roof... The law of God will then be written in their hearts... This is an essential part of the future triumph of Christ and the deliverance of humankind in history and beyond."[2]

This is the Christian vision of the present "kingdom" age that the Trinity planned for our fallen world. How long this blessed period continues once it reaches a predominant state of peace and righteousness, as described by Isaiah and others, is not revealed to us. It could conceivably be compressed into a short time, but more likely will be extended, possibly for thousands of years. Towards this blessed future for the world, Jesus has instructed us to persistently pray "Thy kingdom come, Thy will be done" and to faithfully work, "Go and make disciples of all nations...." Future generations will someday live in Christ's kingdom manifested on earth, as envisioned by Isaiah and the prophets. *The zeal of the Lord Almighty will accomplish this* (Isaiah 9:7).

---

[2] Dallas Willard, *Divine Conspiracy*, page 142

Chapter 9:
The Last Battle: The Final Defeat of Satan and the Destruction of Evil

Our cause is never more in danger than when a human, no longer desiring, but still intending, to do our enemy's [God's] will, looks round upon a universe from which every trace of him seems to have vanished, and asks why he has been forsaken, and still obeys.
~ Uncle Screwtape, *The Screwtape Letters,* by C.S. Lewis

The contents of this chapter are construed from my personal reasoning of how and when the power of evil will most likely be destroyed. I offer it as a possibility, hopeful it will stimulate thoughtful conversation.

Although we have no way of knowing how long the kingdom age of peace and righteousness will last, we have been told what will interrupt this blessed period. Towards the close of the age, with the Second Coming and the consummation of all things just over the horizon, "Satan will be released from prison and will go out to deceive the nations in the four corners of the earth" (Revelation 20:7-8).

One of the most peculiar events in Scripture is the release of Satan from the Abyss. After millennia of sacrifice and suffering by believers – after patiently waiting for the fruition of the kingdom promises and the manifestation of the discipleship of all nations – and then, following hundreds, possibly thousands of years of peace, justice and prosperity – why would God allow Satan to once again inflict his malice upon Christ's people and the world?

Revelation 20 does not say that Satan will be released in response to something the Church does or does not do – such as a new worldwide apostasy. There is no evidence that believers will abandon their discipleship and choose to no longer "obey everything I have commanded you." Of the possible answers, one remains consistent with the fulfillment of the Great Commission and with Isaiah's vision of a mature kingdom towards the end of the present age. **By releasing Satan from prison, Jesus will set in motion events that will lead to the ultimate destruction of evil as it is conquered *spiritually* with the participation of Christ's faithful bride, the new Eve.** The powers of darkness will be finally vanquished as Jesus draws the age to a close and delivers the kingdom to the Father.

What does it mean to conquer evil as found in an immortal being like Satan? Our knowledge is limited, but we can surmise that spiritual evil cannot be eliminated by the exile of its host, even in a Lake of Fire. Paul wrote that our struggle is not against flesh and blood, but against the spiritual forces of evil in the heavenly realms. Evil cannot be rounded up and imprisoned as if it were a material entity limited by physical constraints. It must be destroyed *spiritually* with spiritual weapons.

Chapter 9: The Last Battle: The Final Defeat of Satan and the Destruction of Evil

To gain insight into a possible reason for the devil's release, we first consider the book of Job. Then we will go back to the Garden of Eden.

Revelation does not mention the particulars concerning Satan's resurgence, but Job's story provides an interesting perspective from which to contemplate what might happen.

> Then the Lord said to Satan, "Have you considered my servant Job? There is no one on earth like him; he is blameless and upright, a man who fears God and shuns evil."
> "Does Job fear God for nothing?" Satan replied. "Have you not put a hedge around him and his household and everything he has? You have blessed the work of his hands... But stretch out your hand and strike everything he has, and he will surely curse you to your face."
> The Lord said to Satan, "Very well, then, everything he has is in your hands, but on the man himself do not lay a finger" (Job 1:8-12).
> Then the Lord said to Satan, "He still maintains his integrity..."
> "Skin for skin!" Satan replied. "A man will give all he has for his own life. But stretch out your hand and strike his flesh and bones, and he will surely curse you to your face."
> The Lord said to Satan, "Very well, then, he is in your hands..." (Job 2:3-5).

A similar New Testament account is given when Jesus says to Peter, "Simon, Simon, Satan has asked to sift you as wheat. But I have prayed for you, Simon, that your faith may not fail" (Luke 22:31).

Now forward to Satan's release as the end of the present age approaches. The following is offered as a possible scenario based on Job's example.

A Parable of the Devil's Release
by
David Kullberg

At an unknown time in the future, Satan, who was bound with a great chain and locked away, is brought before the throne of Jesus. When Satan arrives Jesus takes him to a very high mountain and shows him all the kingdoms of the world and their splendor.

Jesus speaks first, looking out across the great expanse. "Look at all the nations of the world – how they obey all that the Father asks. See the wolf and the lion with the playful child? They will neither harm nor destroy, for the earth is full of the knowledge of the Lord as the waters cover the sea."

When Satan does not answer, Jesus looks directly at him and continues, "There is peace in the world. Justice rules the nations. People enjoy the work of their hands and no longer do they bear children doomed to misfortune. The hungry are fed. The blind can see. The prisoners have been set free."

Satan finally speaks, still gazing out towards the world. "They don't love you. You've purchased their loyalty and locked me away. You've made certain they have no other choice."

Chapter 9: The Last Battle: The Final Defeat of Satan and the Destruction of Evil

The devil's gaze gradually moves towards Jesus until their eyes meet. Malice is revealed in Satan's icy stare. He continues, "Just as in the past, the vast majority of humans will still choose me if given the chance."

Satan pauses as he studies his opponent. Jesus shows no emotion other than the hint of a wry grin.

The devil turns away and says, "You have the power to lock me away, but that doesn't make your claim to the throne legitimate. I know you hear my voice. Even if you send me to the Lake of Fire you will still hear me proclaim that I am the one your creatures would choose to rule the kingdoms of this world. All the angels of the Abyss know you have abused your power. You created humans to freely choose – and you and I both know they would choose me."

Their eyes meet again as Satan waits.

Jesus calmly responds, "I believe that most of them have already made their choice, voluntarily, of their own free will."

Satan lightly scoffs, "Test them. Take away their peace and prosperity. And as they did once before in Jerusalem, they will surely curse you to your face."

The ironic grin returns to Jesus' expression. After a thoughtful pause he answers, "Very well, then, they are in your hands."

Satan takes a few steps back. When the meaning of what he has just heard sinks in, a cruel sneer reflects his scorn. He has been given an opening.

He has dealt with weak, pathetic humans before. This time will be no different.

With grotesque confidence, the devil descends the mountain to gather his demonic legions for the last battle.

The Stage is Set

Besides the story of Job, another perspective for considering the meaning of Satan's release comes from the Garden of Eden. Adam, the first man, and Eve, his bride, failed to remain faithful to the Lord when tempted by the serpent, the devil. Now the second Adam, the last Adam (1 Corinthians 15:45), Jesus, awaits his new bride – the redeemed sons and daughters of Eve. Will the new bride shine and pass the test? Or will she also fall prey to deception?

The stage is set for Satan to unleash his wrath upon God's people. Common grace is lifted and an open hostility towards Christ's kingdom begins to surface. Satan no longer bothers with the pretense of utopia or a universal humanistic faith. The weeds start to separate themselves from the wheat. Rebellious men and women unite with demons in their rebellion against God. Satan uses the weapons of his warfare to once again draw those not "sealed" (Revelation 7:3) into the darkness of his bidding and to enlist them in his assault on God's people.

Although there are varying interpretations of Revelation, from this author's perspective, the battle is ultimately spiritual in nature, primarily involving

Satan and his demonic legends. Descriptions like "Gog and Magog," "sand on the seashore," "marching" and "surrounding the camp" may have some physical application, but they are most likely symbolic of spiritual warfare. The common New Testament usage of military metaphors reminds us to be wary of interpreting the symbolism of Revelation 20 as literal military combat against "flesh and blood" (Ephesians 6:12).

The battle is worldwide, not isolated to a literal Jerusalem located in Israel. From Hebrews 12, "You have not come to a mountain that can be touched.... But you have come to Mount Zion, to the heavenly Jerusalem, the city of the living God." The "new Jerusalem" is wherever Christ reigns, wherever the kingdom of God is manifested. Therefore, the entire "four corners of the earth" (Revelation 20:7), wherever Christians are found, will become the battleground for Satan's final confrontation with the believers in Christ.

Repeating an important point, Revelation does not say that Satan's release and the last battle are the consequence of apostasy on the part of believers. Thus the question of why the bride of Christ has to endure this final tribulation is perplexing until we realize that **believers have one final task to perform. There is one last victory to achieve. It is not enough that evil is constrained. The power of darkness must be broken. In order for spiritual evil to be destroyed, the agents of evil must first be released from the Abyss and brought into the battle.**

In Revelation 12:11, John heard a voice from heaven proclaim one of the most prophetic messages in Scripture. "They triumphed over him [Satan] by the blood of the Lamb and by the word of their testimony; they did not love their lives so much as to shrink from death." The voice from heaven discloses to John that Satan's spiritual power is destroyed by two actions: 1) "the blood of the Lamb" – Christ's obedience at the cross (Colossians 2:15); and 2) "the word of their testimony."

Testimony is primarily understood as preaching the good news of the Gospel, or sharing one's personal story of salvation and its life-changing impact. These forms of testimony are instrumental in defeating evil, but there's another powerful testimony that we will consider by returning to Job's story.

Job lost everything except his life. His children were killed. His wealth and home were stolen or destroyed. He was afflicted with painful sores from head to foot. And to make matters worse, he was berated by his wife and criticized by his friends.

As he sat among the ashes scraping his sores with broken pottery, thinking of the disasters that had befallen him and wondering where God was in all of this, he was unaware that his struggle was really against Satan. Despite his lack of understanding, **Job's words of faith, his testimony, demolished Satan's claim that Job's devotion to God was purchased by material blessings.** Job said,

speaking of God, "Though He slay me, yet will I trust Him" (Job 13:15 NKJV).

In writing Revelation, John offers few details of Satan's final defeat. But a possible scenario, consistent with what has been developed thus far, continues this account of the battle by extrapolating Job's experience to every believer living at the time of Satan's release.

After the blessed period of peace and prosperity, when Satan is released, the body of believers will withstand an intense tribulation. How long the time, or how severe the persecution, we are not told. But I doubt it will be any longer or more severe than is necessary for **the bride of Christ to demonstrate her faithfulness to her betrothed**.

Believers will undoubtedly suffer during this time. Many will be pushed to the edge of despair. They will "look round upon a universe from which every trace of God seems to have vanished, and ask why they have been forsaken" (C.S. Lewis). Yet as the redeemed sons and daughters of Eve struggle to hold on against the assault of Satan's fury, Christ's plan unfolds as he awaits the faithful testimony of his bride.

I believe, based on Revelation 12:11, that the testimony will come. The bride of Christ, in one voice, will cry out in defiance of tribulation and death, **"Though our Father slay us, yet will we trust him. Not our will but thy will be done."**

Then coming to the aid of the believers on earth, "fire came down from heaven and devoured them [the forces of evil]" (Revelation 20:9).

What kind of fire?

First, in regards to the humans who join the powers of darkness in this war against God's people, their deaths will accomplish little towards eliminating spiritual evil (e.g., the Flood). Neither can Satan nor his demons be defeated by physical fire, such as what rained down on Sodom and Gomorrah.

So if Christians hold firm to their testimony as they struggle to survive the onslaught, then what would heaven send to help them win the battle? If the word of their faithful testimony is demolishing Satan's claim that he is the rightful ruler of this world; if believers, of their own free will, continue to stand firm against all of the devil's lies and afflictions; if they do not "shrink from death" but continue to hold true – then what "fire" would heaven send in order to turn the tide and empower God's people to go on the offensive and bring about evil's ultimate defeat?

The answer comes from Acts. "Suddenly a sound like the blowing of a violent wind came from heaven and filled the whole house where they were sitting. They saw what seemed to be tongues of fire that separated and came to rest on each of them" (Acts 2:2-3). On the day of Pentecost, fire came down from heaven, and weak but faithful men became bold spiritual warriors who turned the world upside-down.

Chapter 9: The Last Battle: The Final Defeat of Satan and the Destruction of Evil

During the last battle, the people of God will hold true to their faith. Revelation gives no indication otherwise. As faithful soldiers, they will man their posts and perform their duties. Then the Holy Spirit will rain down upon them as fire from heaven. Greatly empowered, they will go on the offensive, disarming Satan and making a public spectacle of him in front of the rulers, the authorities, the powers of this dark world, and the spiritual forces of evil in the heavenly realms. Jesus said, "He who believes in Me, the works that I do, he will do also; and greater works than these he will do; because I go to the Father" (John 14:12 NASV).

I have even considered the delightful possibility that, by the powerful presence of the Holy Spirit, the world may witness many conversions from amongst the remaining nonbelievers as a final display of God's grace and the utter ruin of Satan's kingdom.

By the joyful testimonies of the saints, especially after enduring incredible suffering, spiritual darkness will be vanquished as a brilliant light illuminates the world from a great multitude of individual sources. Satan will be crushed, discredited and powerless. He will have no fight left and no place to hide. His minions will follow him into the Lake of Fire to accuse him forever. The great dragon will be conquered and the power of evil eternally destroyed. The marriage supper of the Lamb awaits the victorious, faithful bride.

> Then the end will come, when he hands over the kingdom to God the Father after he has

destroyed all dominion, authority, and power. For he must reign until he has put all his enemies under his feet. The last enemy to be destroyed is death (1 Corinthians 15:24-26).

Chapter 10:
How to Live in This Story

The Story Summary

1. Life is not a cruel hoax, but rather a raging war to defeat evil with good. Job's story, when viewed from God's perspective, reveals that the events and circumstances of life, often feeling like combat, set the stage for faithful believers to shine a brilliant light that pierces the very heart of darkness. As a result, the Kingdom of God continues its rise towards predominance on earth as it is in heaven.

2. God began his creation with the end in mind. If there had been a better way for God to create eternal men and women with whom to share eternity, then we would be living in that story instead of this one. We are no more intended to remain a creature of the dust than is a butterfly to remain a caterpillar.

3. God allowed evil to enter his creation; he uses it for his purposes. His children will enter eternity with knowledge of the consequences of sin embedded in their memories forever.

4. Jesus possesses all power and authority. He will establish his rule from heaven until all of his enemies are defeated. He will come back to earth after he has won the victory, not in order to win it.

5. Jesus, the rightful king, is presently overturning the City of Man's control of the world while permeating a corrupted world with the reality of his kingdom.

6. Satan has joined the battle, giving the City of Man his power, and throne, and great authority. The false church offers salvation through secular culture and social action. Collective consciousness is pursued and enforced. The spirit of Babylon, the world system, seduces rulers and peoples with counterfeit promises of peace, prosperity and an earthly paradise apart from God.

7. Judgment has fallen, is falling, and will fall on Babylon throughout history. God is continuously shaking the world. In his time, he will break Babylon's spell and clear the way for the kingdom's eventual predominance.

8. The Great Commission and the kingdom promises will continue to materialize, signaling the advance of God's kingdom from insignificance to predominance. The kingdom will grow as it is advanced by the Holy Spirit and lived faithfully by believers. Once it reaches maturity on the earth, the blessings of the kingdom age will impart a true peace, prosperity and healing to the nations – to both Christians and non-believers alike.

9. Towards the end of the kingdom age, Satan will be released from the Abyss. In a final battle against God's people, he is defeated and evil is

destroyed by the faithful testimony of believers greatly empowered by the Holy Spirit. Jesus will then return for his faithful bride and deliver the kingdom to the Father.

Where We Are in the Story

Christians on earth are presently living with the turmoil of continual spiritual warfare (Chapters 5 and 6). Although the kingdom continues to grow throughout this period, the City of Man appears to be in control. The leaders of the City of Man are committed to their quest of a united world order independent of any Christian deity. They have embraced the seductive dream of "Babylon," the world system, and the creation of a man-centered, utopian paradise.

Whenever the spirit of Babylon has established corporeal control of governance in the past, the consequences have been devastating for God's people and civil society. Twentieth Century examples of utopian experiments were Soviet communism under Lenin/Stalin (approximately 25 million killed), Chinese communism under Mao (approximately 40 million killed), and Nazi Germany under Hitler (approximately 6 million killed plus millions more in World War II). The rulers of these "new world orders" justified these deaths as necessary, or even required, in order to impose their earthly paradise.

Dietrich Bonhoeffer, a German pastor in the 1920s and 30s, tried to warn God's people about the evil lying just beneath the surface of the National

Socialist (Nazi) movement. Rationalizations, compromise and even good intentions caused believers to overlook and, at times, support the prevailing spirit. The spirit of Babylon, taking bodily form in the government of Hitler and the Nazis, promised compelling solutions to what seemed to be insurmountable problems. (The people were exhausted from economic malaise and social chaos.) Because German Christians failed to heed the warnings, it was too late by the time they realized the truth. The spirit had consolidated its physical formation and was able to manifest substantial power to enforce its will.

We live in critical times. **In America, we are experiencing a new Tower of Babel rising from the shadows. Veiled in deception and lies, disguised as false promises of prosperity, tolerance and security, the seductive spirit of Babylon is once again seeking to gain a physical presence.** This time it is described as Progressive socialism. Initiated in the United States a hundred years ago, **Progressivism is a social revolution no longer content to hide behind political liberalism**. The progressives recruit as allies anyone who opposes limited constitutional government and a Christ-centered view of culture, personal responsibility and the sanctity of life. Those who fail to join are considered enemies of their utopian vision. Christians and others who value individual liberty and oppose a coercive tyranny of "collective consciousness" are already being accused of subverting their illusory dream.

If the spiritual Babylon is able to establish an operational reality in America, it will intimidate and eventually persecute those who refuse to submit. God will once again bring judgment and cause this new Tower of Babel to collapse, just as he has destroyed all the Babels of history. But in the process, there will be much turmoil, suffering and tribulation.

Believers and those who value America's founding principles must not wait until the spirit takes on a clearly visible formation. The time is short, but it is not too late for America. We owe it to our children and grandchildren to not ignore the lessons of history. The freedom to practice our faith outside the four walls of the church, and to teach our children as we choose, will be among the first of many rights to disappear if we allow a statist utopian experiment to capture our nation.

Living Faithfully in the Story

Although many Americans are becoming aware that our country is headed down a dangerous path, there is much confusion about what action to take. Fortunately, Scripture instructs us how to integrate the spiritual battle against the world system of Babylon into our daily lives. But initially we must categorically reject the enemy's deceptive assertion that the spiritual and material worlds operate independently. As stated before, there is no sacred/secular divide. This is simply a lie leading to confusion and futility.

Throughout history God has had to purify his Church by separating his people from the ways of the world. As God did through the prophets for ancient Israel, he still does through the Holy Spirit today. He admonishes us to reject Babylon. In Revelation 18:4 he says, "Come out of her, my people, so that you will not share in her sins, so that you will not receive any of her plagues…"

As discussed in Chapter 7, by "come out of her" the Lord does not intend for us to retreat into an earthly fortress or hide in the woods. Rather, we seek to live in Christ's kingdom now, in the midst of a hostile world, because God is our fortress. Our responsibility is to turn from a compromised life within the world system.

Another instruction comes from a familiar verse, 2 Chronicles 7:14, and echoes the command to "come out." With the important lead-in of verse 13, God said, "When I shut up the heavens so that there is no rain, or command locusts to devour the land or send a plaque among my people, (14) **if *my people*, who are called by my name, will humble themselves and pray and seek my face and *turn from* their wicked ways, then will I hear from heaven and will forgive their sin and will heal their land.**"

This is more than a significant promise. In the present state of our nation, it is a critical offer from God that we cannot afford to miss. By "turn from their wicked ways" (i.e., repent), God does not mean just personal moral sins, which are included, but are not exclusive. There are other types of sin, subtle compromises with the world system that are often overlooked.

The Lord commands us to demolish strongholds (which include the pillars of the anti-Christ, humanistic City of Man). This is accomplished by taking every thought captive to the obedience of Christ – which includes not just our inner lives, but also every thought about government, education, economics, business and technology, law, science and health, media and the arts, and all areas of life and culture. Why? Because Biblical wisdom is the highest love for human flourishing and for overcoming evil with good.

Although we know we will not perfectly obey God this side of eternity, it should not prevent us from being committed to the pursuit of obedience. As Martin Luther said, "Where the battle rages – precisely that little point which the world and the devil are at that moment attacking – there the loyalty of the soldier is proved."

Demolishing strongholds that are empowered by the spirit of Babylon is not accomplished by social strife, political coercion or physical force. We are to use the weapons of our warfare. While praying "Thy kingdom come, thy will be done," we ask the Lord to identify these strongholds. Then we are to reject them, eliminating them from our lives and from whatever domain over which we have authority. The "coming out of" the world system is completed when the stronghold is replaced with something that reflects our love for the Lord. *"If you love me, you will obey what I command" (John 14:15).*

There are far reaching blessings to a nation when believers *turn from* the world system and *demolish strongholds* by creating a new culture grounded on a firm foundation. Taking every thought captive results not only in the renewing of one's mind; it also brings renewal to America.

Concerning implementation, believers are not called to take over the world's culture or to imitate it with a Christian spin. **We are to create something new and vibrant, which embodies the reality of the Lord's truth, beauty and goodness.** When we embrace Christ's reign on earth as it is in heaven, and turn away from our misguided conformity to the world system, then we can lay hold of what John promised. "This is the confidence we have in approaching God: that if we ask anything according to his will, he hears us" (1 John 5:14).

Epilogue

It feels as if we live in a world in which a brood of moral vipers has been hatched that are waiting to unleash themselves on the world. But let me make myself clear. All attempts to restore or protect the values and morals that have made this nation great will be in vain without the restoration of a vital Evangelical Christianity.

If you are of such a character that you want the best for your country, the time to hesitate is past. It is time to count the cost and decide what needs to be done to enable you to be the most effective person you can be in the renewal of the moral and spiritual life of the nation. The one who takes this attitude is the true patriot.
~ William Wilberforce, *Real Christianity*

Appendix A:
Interpreting Biblical Metaphors

Thousand years. The millennial is taken literally by some as 1,000 actual years, **while others interpret it metaphorically as a long but undetermined period of time**[3] (e.g., a thousand years, 2 Peter 3:8; a thousand generations, Psalm 105:8; a thousand hills, Psalm 50:10).

Babylon the Great. According to some, it is used in Revelation for Rome as the center of opposition to God and his people. To others, **it represents the whole political and religious system of the world in general**. To still others, it is understood as a literal Babylon – rebuilt and restored.[4]

Beast coming out of the sea. According to some, the beast symbolizes the Roman empire, **the deification of secular authority**. To others, he is the final, personal antichrist.[5]

Another beast, coming out of the earth. According to some, **he symbolizes religious power in the service of secular authorities**. To others, he is the personal false prophet.[6]

Last Days. According to the NIV study notes, "**The 'last days' include all the days between Christ's**

---

[3] The NIV Study Bible, General Editor, Kenneth Barker (Grand Rapids, MI., Zondervan, 1995, 10th Anniversary Edition) pg. 1946
[4] NIV, pg 1940
[5] NIV, pg 1939
[6] NIV, pg 1939

first and second comings, and is another way of saying 'from now on.'"[7]

Acts 2:16-17. (Peter, on the day of Pentecost, quoting Joel 2:28-29), "This is what was spoken by the prophet Joel: '**In the last days**, God says, I will pour out my Spirit on all people...'"

Hebrews 1:1-2. "In the past God spoke to our forefathers through the prophets at many times and in various ways, **but in these last days** he has spoken to us by his Son, whom he appointed heir of all things..."

Bold highlights have been added to emphasize the definition favored in this text.

---

[7] The NIV Life Application Study Bible, General Editor, Ronald A Beers (Grand Rapids, MI. Zondervan, 1983, pg. 1946

Appendix B:
Attributes of the World System

- Prosperity through debt.
- Unity through coercion.
- Improving life for some through the death of others.
- Security through dependency.
- Peace through war.
- Equality through mediocrity.
- Social coherency through oppressive control.
- Persuasion through deceit.
- Salvation through collective consciousness.

The "golden rule" of the world system: The end justifies the means – whatever action is deemed necessary in order to achieve the desired result is considered sanctified by good intentions. Therefore, a perceived benefit to some can justify injustice done to others.

Appendix C:
The Kingdom's Growth to Predominance is Not a Theocracy

To seek first the Kingdom of God is to pray and act for the fulfillment of the request, "Thy will be done on earth as it is in heaven." We must ask ourselves: Is what Jesus instructed us to seek really going to happen? How will the kingdom grow in the world?

It is true that each individual believer has as much right as any other citizen to advocate for his or her conscience and moral values. But the actual Kingdom of God on earth is not a religious system or a set of principles to be institutionalized and then systematically imposed upon the broader society.

Rather, the Kingdom is a living stream (a stream of life) – interactive, guiding, permeating the world with the revelation of Jesus Christ, the Truth. Not forcing old things to change, but making all things new. Not spiritual versus material, but an invisible presence intent on physical manifestation. Not magical or instant, but a hard-fought, ongoing transformation empowered by an indwelling spiritual life. Grounded by obedience and trust. Purified in the fires of suffering and perseverance. Flourishing in love and forgiveness. A "new Jerusalem," the light of life, rising from the dark shadows of a world consumed with death.

Jesus did not come to destroy God's world, but to usher in a new history – a new story of victory with God's people as the central characters.

As to the matter of theocracy, individual believers responding voluntarily to the spiritual kingdom will not replace divinely ordained civil government with another institution such as the church. This false but common accusation is often made by critics wishing to mischaracterize the kingdom. The organizational church has its own distinct requirements under God that do not include civil government.

The groups most likely to cry "theocracy" whenever a Christian speaks in public are the progressives, liberals, and social gospel adherents of the religious left. Yet these are the groups that consistently rely upon the power of government to enforce their own social agendas. In contrast, the Bible prescribes very limited responsibilities for any central government.

The Gospel affects change in society from the bottom up, through revival and personal transformation empowered by the Holy Spirit. Loving God and obeying his Word can only occur voluntarily, respecting each individual's conscience, one person at a time. The qualities of the Kingdom of God are self-government and personal responsibility, not force, manipulation or political coercion. The growing influence of the kingdom in the world will gradually eliminate the need for extensive civil government. That is why the growing manifestation of the kingdom will lead to increased freedom. "Now the Lord is the Spirit, and where the Spirit of the Lord is, there is freedom" (2 Corinthians 3:17).

God's way of moving toward the future is, with gentle persistence in unfailing purpose, to bring about the transformation of the human heart by speaking with human beings and living with and in them.... It is this millennia-long process that Jesus the Son of man brings, and will bring, to completion.... All of the instruments of brutality and deceit that human government and society now employ to manage a corrupted and unruly humanity will then have no use.... Thus we see repeatedly portrayed in prophecy the gentleness of this government – for the first time a completely adequate government, in which the means to the good do not limit or destroy the possibility of goodness.
~ Dallas Willard, *Divine Conspiracy*

Appendix D:
Three Common Theological Views of the Millennium

Postmillennialism. The view of the last things which holds that the Kingdom of God is now being extended in the world through the preaching of the Gospel and the saving work of the Holy Spirit, that the world eventually will be Christianized, and that the return of Christ will occur at the close of a long period of righteousness and peace commonly called the *Millennium*.

This view is, of course, to be distinguished from that optimistic but false view of human betterment and progress held by Modernists and Liberals which teaches that the Kingdom of God on earth will be achieved through a natural process by which mankind will be improved and social institutions will be reformed and brought to a higher level of culture and efficiency. This latter view... regards the Kingdom of God as the product of natural laws in an evolutionary process.[8]

Loraine Boettner. What will [Christ] be able to do in a 1000 year millennium, seated on a throne in Jerusalem [premillennialism], that He cannot do now? He already has **all authority**, **all power**, in heaven and on earth. He can never have any more... than he has now. He commanded his followers to go **now**, and **make disciples of all the nations**.... It cannot mean a merely superficial

---

[8] Dr. J.G. Vos quoted by Loraine Boettner, The Millennium (Phillipsburg, N.J.: P&R, 1957) pg. 4

announcement of the Gospel to those nations, as some say, but a truly effective Christianizing of the world.[9]

Postmillennialists, as opposed to amillennialists or premillennialists, believe that the Great Commission will actually be fulfilled by the power of the Holy Spirit as all the nations of the world become disciples of Christ, seeking to obey his word. They also believe that Jesus will come again after he has won the victory, not in order to win it.

Amillennialism. The view of the last things which holds that the Bible does not predict a *Millennium* or period of worldwide peace and righteousness on this earth before the end of the world. Amillennialism teaches that there will be a parallel and contemporaneous development of good and evil – God's kingdom and Satan's kingdom – in this world, which will continue until the second coming of Christ. At the second coming of Christ the resurrection and judgment will take place, followed by the eternal order of things.[10]

Premillennialism (Dispensational). The church will ultimately lose influence in the world and become corrupted or apostate toward the end of the church age. Christ will return secretly to rapture his saints before the great tribulation. After the tribulation, Christ will return to earth to administer

---

[9] Loraine Boettner, The Millennium (Phillipsburg, N.J.: P&R, 1957) pg. 409

[10] Dr. J. G. Vos quoted by Loraine Boettner, The Millennium (Phillipsburg, N.J.: P&R, 1957) pg. 4

a Jewish political kingdom based in Jerusalem for one thousand years. Satan will be bound, and the temple will be rebuilt and the sacrificial system reinstituted. Near the end of the millennium, Satan will be released and Christ will be attacked at Jerusalem. Christ will call down judgment from heaven and destroy his enemies. The (second) resurrection and the judgment of the wicked will occur, initiating the eternal order.[11]

---

[11] Kenneth Gentry, He Shall Have Dominion, quoted by R.C. Sproul, The Last Days According to Jesus (Grand Rapids, MI.: Baker Books, 1998) pg. 197 (Gentry is a postmillennialist.)

Acknowledgements

Recalling the C.S. Lewis quote in the introduction, my "fellow-pupil" approach – writing as "one amateur to another…comparing notes" – would not have been possible without the enlightenment provided by this partial list of biblical scholars and theologians who have influenced my writing: Dallas Willard, Matthew Henry, St. Augustine, Jonathan Edwards, C.S. Lewis, John Calvin, Charles Spurgeon, Marcellus Kik, R.J. Rushdoony, Jacques Ellul, Francis Schaeffer, Herbert Schlossberg, Gary DeMar, N.T. Wright, Loraine Boettner, Kenneth Gentry, and R.C. Sproul.

The contents of Chapter 8, "The Last Battle: The Final Defeat of Satan and the Destruction of Evil," are construed from my personal reasoning of how and when the power of evil will most likely be destroyed. It is offered as a possibility in the hope that this will stimulate thoughtful conversation and faithful action.

The War Against God

A novel by David Kullberg

Rich in romance and political intrigue, a globalist billionaire and his ingenious mistress orchestrate their strategy of a new world order. To succeed, they must confuse, deceive and overcome a powerful opponent – evangelical Christianity. The deception will threaten not only the Church, but the very meaning of the Gospel. Risking all, a circle of courageous young friends enters the conflict, unwilling to lose the faith and nation they love.

Facebook: The War Against God
Website: http://waragainstgod.com
Available in Paperback (6x9) and Ebook
Available at: Amazon.com and BN.com (Barnes & Noble)

Excerpt from book review by Bill Blankschaen @ Patheos.com:

> Make no mistake, The War Against God depicts a battle of worldviews, but in a tangible way that tugs at the heart as much as at the mind. Kullberg clearly spent time developing the mix of characters who share an authentic depth often missing from Christian fiction. That's not to say that all ends well. This isn't a sanitized sitcom with halos and white robes all around. For example, the tension between the humanist Connelly and his Christian son, a U.S. Congressman who risks much to resist his

father, seems to typify the incongruity of the two worldviews and how vast the gulf between them.

Nor do all live happily ever after, and certainly not without some scars. Explosive action, seductive relationships, subterfuge, harrowing kidnappings, cold-blooded murder, passionate romance, life-transforming repentance — all these fit into Kullberg's riveting tale as if they each had a place within the Christian worldview. And they do.

The War Against God is an intelligent, intellectually stimulating safari across the wide savanna of ways our worldviews affect all areas of life — politics, genetics, prophecy, psychology, media, love and relationships, to name just a few.

CPSIA information can be obtained
at www.ICGtesting.com
Printed in the USA
FFOW05n1711170115

9 780988 432130